KL RAHUL COLOUR

INDIAN CRICKETER

MR VIVEK KUMAR PANDEY SHAMBHUNATH

ISBN 979-888530804-5

Short biography of Kl Rahul and about life .During writing this book no character & no religious are harmed written by Mr Vivek Kumar Pandey. winner youngest writer award 1st rank in india 2020.He is only one writer can publish 700+ own book that was greatest successfull in his life.

Contents

Foreword

Author biography in English :MY NAME IS VIVEK KUMAR PANDEY . I WAS BORN IN 30 SEP 2002,I AM FROM SURAT GUJARAT INDIA.MY DREAM WAS TO BE GOOD WRITERS ,MY FAMILY SUPPORTED ME TO SUCCESSFUL AND I CAN DO IT MY SELF.How do I write? That is a question, I believe, that cannot be honestly answered by me."CELEBRATING YOUNGEST WRITER AWARD WINNER IN GUJARAT 1ST RANK" MR PANDEY JI . I may think I did a good job writing something when in reality it could be horrible. The reader is the one who decides the quality of my writing. I do not find writing to be natural to me and therefore find it to be a real challenge. My trick as a challenged writer is to do the best I can and know that I am happy with the final outcome. It may take a while to do my best and there may be quite a few problems I run into along the way.

I am not a greedy person those who are thinking about me and my self I never tried it anyone people suffering from sadness ,I trying to get promoted people suffering from happiness and joy in your Life Time. Now in current situation in India and also world people are unemployed and have no many but our indian governor help to people to get free food from ration card , i also take part in leadership team ,i am Motivational speaker , Film script writer. There was my two dream firstly writer and secondly actor & also my own film is upcoming soon i done almost completely completed script for my film .I AM GOING TO SAY WORD OF HEART TOUCH OUT PLEASE READ IT" , firstly i thanks my father he supports me in this field they always getting inspired me by own his words and behavior ,they always said that he was a biggest person in the world in future and also they purchase fruit and chocolate for me in anytime & anyway , firstly my father buy him then call me Vivek you want a chocolate i will say yes papa but how many tell me ,papa: you tell me how much i buy him i told 1 or 2 chocolate but my father purchase whole the boxes of chocolate and they get suprised me. MY FATHER WAS BORN IN " 20 SEPTEMBER" 1971 IN INDIA.

1) MY FATHER FAVORITE CLOTHES IS KURTA PAIJMA AND ALSO STYLES SHOE

2) FAVORITE SINGER IS KISHORE DA

3) FAVORITE STATE GUJARAT AND KOLKATA , HIS VILLAGE IN BIHAR

4) FAVORITE COLOR BLACK AND WHITE

THEY ALSO LOVE cricket like IPL and one day t-20 .they also like watching a News daily and heard the song daily ,they also interested in tik tok video but in current time tik tok is banned in india but also few videos are in you tube. In lockdown time my family and me very enjoy day daily. my father play daily ludo with his sister and son, daughter.they always loved tea and coffee anytime call me "। विवेक थोड़ा चाय बनाओना विवेक तुम्हारे हाथ का चाय अच्छा लगता है". I make it tea for my father but some reason after the April to june they are suffering from fever and cough , weakness on 6 June 2020 my father death. they not told me say bye bye his life. After death of 6 June on 10 june my mom and dad anniversary.but my father is Best in the world they can do anything for me please take care of father and respect it of your parents.

CHAPTER ONE

Kl Rahul Colour

- KL Rahul

1. During writing this book no character & no religious are harmed written by Mr Vivek Kumar Pandey.

Kannur Lokesh Rahul (born 18 April 1992) is an Indian international cricketer who is the vice-captain of the India national cricket team in One Day Internationals and Twenty20 Internationals. He plays for Karnataka in domestic cricket and captains Punjab Kings in the Indian Premier League. He is a right-handed batsman and an occasional wicket-keeper.

Rahul made his international debut in 2014 and scored his maiden Test century in his second Test match. He was the first Indian to score a century on One Day International debut, and the third Indian to score a century in all three formats of international cricket.

- *Early life*

KL Rahul was born on 18 April 1992 to KN Lokesh and Rajeshwari in Bangalore. His father Lokesh, who was born in Kananur, Magadi taluk, is a professor and former director at the National Institute of Technology Karnataka (NITK) in Mangalore. His mother Rajeshwari is a professor at Mangalore University. Lokesh, who was a fan of the cricketer Sunil Gavaskar, wanted to name his son after Gavaskar's, but mistook Rohan Gavaskar's name as Rahul.

Rahul grew up in Mangalore, completing his high school at NITK English Medium School and pre-university at St. Aloysius College.He started cricket training at the age of 10, and, two years later, started playing matches for both Bangalore United Cricket Club and his club in Mangalore. At age 18 he moved to Bangalore to study at Jain University and pursue his cricket career.

- *Domestic career*

Rahul made his first-class cricket debut for Karnataka in the 2010–11 season. In the same season he represented his country at the 2010 ICC Under-19 Cricket World Cup, scoring a total of 143 runs in the competition.[citation needed] He made his debut in the Indian Premier League in 2013, for Royal Challengers Bangalore.During the 2013–14 domestic season he scored 1,033 first-class runs, the second highest scorer that season.

Playing for South Zone in the final of the 2014–15 Duleep Trophy against Central Zone, Rahul scored 185 off 233 balls in the first innings and 130 off 152 in the second. He was named the player of the match and selection to the Indian Test squad for the Australian tour followed.

Returning home after the Test series, Rahul became Karnataka's first triple-centurion, scoring 337 against Uttar Pradesh. He went on to score 188 in the 2014–15 Ranji Trophy final against Tamil Nadu and finished the season with an average of 93.11 in the nine matches he played.

- *International career*

- K.L. Rahul practicing in nets (2019)

Rahul made his Test debut in the 2014 Boxing Day Test at the Melbourne Cricket Ground. He replaced Rohit Sharma and was presented with his Test cap by MS Dhoni. He batted at number six and made three runs in the first innings; in the second innings, he played at number 3 and made only 1 run but retained his place for the next Test at Sydney where he opened the innings with Murali Vijay and made 110 runs, his maiden international hundred.

He was part of the 15-man squad for the Indian tour of Bangladesh in June 2015 but withdrew due to Dengue fever. He returned to the side for the first Test of the Sri Lankan tour after Murali Vijay was ruled out due to injury, scoring his second Test century and being named player of the match. During the match he kept wicket after Wriddhiman Saha was injured.

He was named in the squad to tour Zimbabwe in 2016 and made his One Day International (ODI) debut against Zimbabwe at Harare Sports Club, scoring a century on debut - the first Indian cricketer to do so on debut.He made his Twenty20 International (T20I) debut later in the same tour.

He was picked in the Indian squad for the four-test tour against West Indies in 2016. Rahul played in the second Test at Jamaica and scored a strokeful 158, his highest Test score then. In the process, he became the first Indian opener to score a century in his debut Test in the West Indies.In the first match of the T20I series in the United States, he scored a century off 46 balls in a losing cause, the second-fastest ever and fastest by an Indian.He also set the world record for being the only player to score hundred in first innings as opener in both Tests and ODIs.

Lokesh Rahul set the record for the fastest batsman to have scored centuries in all three formats in just 20 innings surpassing the record of Ahmed Shehzad who took 76 innings. He is the first player in T20I history to score a century (110*) while batting at number 4 position or lower. On 3 July 2018, Rahul smashed his second T20 International ton against England. He is also the first Indian batsman to be dismissed hit-wicket in T20Is.

On 11 January 2019, Hardik Pandya and K. L. Rahul were suspended by the Board of Control for Cricket in India (BCCI) following controversial comments they made on the Indian talk show Koffee with Karan earlier in the month. They were both sent home ahead of the ODI series against Australia and the fixtures of India's tour to New Zealand.On 24 January 2019, after lifting the suspension on Pandya and Rahul, the BCCI announced that Rahul would re-join the squad for India A matches.

In April 2019, he was named in India's squad for the 2019 Cricket World Cup. He scored his maiden hundred for India in the World Cup against Sri Lanka. In December 2019, in the first T20I match against the West Indies, Rahul scored his 1,000th run in T20I cricket.

In October 2020, Rahul was named as the vice-captain for the One Day

- *International and Twenty20 International series of India against Australia.*

Rahul had a moderate ODI and T20I series against Australia. He made 77 against Australia in the second ODi and 51 in the 1st T20i .India lost the ODI series by 2-1 but won the T20 series by the same margin. Rahul was included in the test squad for the Border-Gavaskar trophy but was not picked in the playing 11 for the first 2 tests. He injured himself during practice and was ruled out for the remaining tour. As a result, he also missed the home test series against England in Feb 2021. He returned to the national side for the T20 and ODI series against England. However he struggled with the bat. There was a dip in his form in the T20 series as he had scores of 1, 0, 0, 14 before being dropped for the 5th T20. India won the T20 series by 3–2.He returned to form in the ODI series scoring match winning 62* and was involved in a 100 run partnership with debutant Krunal Pandya who scored a 50. He continued his form by scoring 108 runs in the 2nd ODI and was involved in another 100 run partnership with Rishabh Pant.

In September 2021, Rahul was named in India's squad for the 2021 ICC Men's T20 World Cup. He scored the tournament's joint-fastest fifty in just 18 balls, against Scotland.

- *Indian Premier League*

- Rahul with RCB in 2015

Rahul made his Indian Premier League (IPL) debut for Royal Challengers Bangalore (RCB) as a wicket-keeper batsman during the 2013 competition. Ahead of the 2014 IPL, he was bought by the Sunrisers Hyderabad for INR 1 crore, before returning to RCB ahead of the 2016 IPL season. He finished the season as the 11th highest run-scorer, and RCB's third, with 397 runs from 14 matches. For his performances in the 2016 IPL season, he was named as wicket keeper in the Cricinfo and Cricbuzz IPL XI. Rahul missed the 2017 season due to a shoulder injury.

In the 2018 IPL Auction, he was bought by Kings XI Punjab (now Punjab Kings) for INR 11 crore, the joint-third highest price. In the team's first match of the season he scored the fastest 50 in IPL history, taking 14 balls to reach the milestone and breaking the record of Sunil Narine.] For his performances in the 2018 IPL season, he was named in the Cricinfo and Cricbuzz IPL XI. After making scores of 90+ three times during 2018, he reached his maiden IPL century in 2019, scoring 100 not out from 64 against Mumbai Indians. For his performances in the 2019 IPL season, he was named in the Cricinfo IPL XI.

Rahul was named captain of the Kings XI Punjab for the 2020 IPL, after former captain Ravichandran Ashwin was traded to Delhi Capitals.

In the match against Royal Challengers Bangalore on 24 September 2020, he scored an unbeaten 132 off just 69 balls. With that century, he broke the record of the most runs scored by an Indian batsman in an IPL match. He also broke the record of the most runs scored by a captain in an IPL match.

In the IPL 2020 season, he scored 670 runs in all the 14 matches he played. He scored 5 fifties and 1 hundred with the highest score of an unbeaten 132 against RCB and also had an average of 55.83.

Rahul won the Orange Cap in IPL 2020 for scoring most runs in IPL 2020 (670 runs).He was retained by the Punjab Kings ahead of the 2021 IPL season.He scored 626 runs in IPL 2021, finishing as the team's highest scorer in the season.

CHAPTER TWO

Punjab Kings (IPL TEAM)

- *Punjab Kings*

The Punjab Kings (PBKS) are a franchise cricket team based in Mohali, Punjab, that plays in the Indian Premier League (IPL). Established in 2008 as the Kings XI Punjab (KXIP), the franchise is jointly owned by Mohit Burman, Ness Wadia, Preity Zinta and Karan Paul. The team plays its home matches at the PCA Stadium, Mohali. Since 2010, they also have been playing some of their home games at either Dharamsala or Indore. Apart from the 2014 season when they topped the league table and finished runners-up, the team has made only one other playoff appearance in 13 seasons.

The Punjab Kings played in the now-defunct Champions League Twenty20 once, in 2014 as the Kings XI Punjab and finished as semi-finalists. The team name was changed to Punjab Kings in February 2021.

- *Franchise history*

In 2007, the Board of Control for Cricket in India (BCCI) created the cricket tournament the Indian Premier League, based on the Twenty20 format of the game. Franchises for eight cities were made available in an auction held in Mumbai on 20 February 2008. The team representing Punjab was bought by the Dabur group's Mohit Burman (46%), the Wadia group's Ness Wadia (23%), Preity Zinta

(23%), and Saptarshi Dey of the Dey & Dey Group (minor stake). The group paid a total of $76 million to acquire the franchise.

As the Kings XI Punjab, the franchise's catchment areas were the regions of Kashmir, Jammu, Himachal Pradesh, Punjab and Haryana—evident from the letter sequence "K J H P H" in the banner of the team's logo.

- Expulsion from the IPL and return

Following the controversy surrounding the BCCI and Lalit Modi in 2010, the Indian Premier League announced on 10 October 2010 that it had terminated the franchise contracts of Kings XI Punjab and the Rajasthan Royals. The teams announced that they would take legal action to remain in the Indian Premier League.Initially, the team tried to negotiate a solution with the league, but when one could not be reached, they decided to file a case in Mumbai High Court accusing the IPL of getting rid of the two teams so that when the bidding process would start for the 2012 IPL season, the contract would be given to a more lucrative bidder.

Kings XI Punjab was reinstated with the involvement of the High Court.

- Name change

On 17 February 2021, Kings XI Punjab was renamed to Punjab Kings, ahead of the 2021 Indian Premier League. Ness Wadia explained the reason for changing the franchise name was to "relook at things" and rebrand after 13 seasons of IPL. He expressed his disappointment over the franchise for "not being able to win a title" and expected them to "start afresh" after a name change. He added that the name change had been planned two years ago and COVID-19 had just delayed the announcement.

- Team history

This article needs additional citations for verification. Please help improve this article by adding citations to reliable sources. Unsourced material may be challenged and removed.
Find sources: "Punjab Kings" – news · newspapers · books · scholar · JSTOR (September 2020) (Learn how and when to remove this template message)

- 2008 IPL season

The 2008 tournament got off to a slow start for the Kings XI Punjab, with the team losing their first two games. However, 94 runs by Kumar Sangakkara helped them to win the third game. Despite the absence of Brett Lee and Simon Katich (who were committed to tour the West Indies with Australia), the team found its groove. Powered by their balanced bowling line-up and effective top order, the team won nine of its next 10 matches, clinching a berth in the semi-final, where their run in the tournament came to an end with a comprehensive nine-wicket loss to the Chennai Super Kings.

Shaun Marsh was arguably KXIP's star player in the inaugural IPL. The opener from Western Australia was overlooked in the IPL player auctions and was signed by the franchise on 9 April.He finished the tournament as the Orange Cap holder—the award for the player with the most runs across the competition—with an average of 68.44 and a strike rate of 139.68 in 11 innings. Marsh managed to hit one century and five half-centuries across the course of the tournament.

- 2009 IPL season

Finishing as semi-finalists in 2008, Kings XI Punjab started with ambitions to win the trophy. These were supported by their new sponsors Emirates. With two available slots to fill, the Kings XI Punjab made bids on Jerome Taylor and Yusuf Abdulla at the second IPL auction.

The team took a hit as most of their Australian cricketers were unavailable. The team lacked available pace bowlers after Jerome Taylor backed out at the last minute with an injury.

The team lost badly to the Delhi Daredevils and the Kolkata Knight Riders (KKR), however, they returned to form by beating the Royal Challengers, the Rajasthan Royals and the Mumbai Indians. Then the team witnessed a roller-coaster ride in their next eight matches with four wins and four losses. The team's semi-final hopes were crushed after losing to the Chennai Super Kings in their last match.

- 2010 IPL season

Kings XI Punjab lost six matches to the Kolkata Knight Riders, the Delhi Daredevils, the Royal Challengers Bangalore, the Deccan Chargers, the Rajasthan Royals and the Mumbai Indians but managed to win a match against Chennai Super Kings when the scores were level and the match went to a Super Over. Kings XI Punjab were boosted by the return of Brett Lee against Kolkata, but he was not at his best. Shaun Marsh returned in the match against the Mumbai Indians. In spite of his good performance, which included a half century, the team lost the match. They ended the 2010 IPL in the last position.

- 2011 IPL season

The 2011 IPL season looked promising when they brought a full strength team with Michael Bevan as coach and Adam Gilchrist appointed as the captain.

Kings XI Punjab missed out on the play offs by two points (or one victory). This meant they finished fifth in the points table.

- 2012 IPL season

Kings XI Punjab finished in sixth place overall, winning eight matches out of sixteen.

- 2013 IPL season

Kings XI Punjab failed to qualify for the play-offs, but batsman David Miller played one of the innings of the tournament in the 51st match against the Royal Challengers Bangalore, as he smashed 101 off 38 deliveries and included eight fours and seven sixes. Coming in at no. 5 when Kings XI Punjab was struggling with only 51 runs in the scoreboard in the eighth over and chasing a target of 190, Miller rectified the game and led Punjab to a six-wicket win with two overs remaining. Adam Gilchrist retired at the end of the season.

- 2014 IPL season

Australia's T20I captain George Bailey was leading the squad for the seventh season. Other buys featured the likes of Virender Sehwag, Glenn Maxwell and Mitchell Johnson. Kings XI Punjab began the tournament by winning their first five games which were held outside India in UAE due to the general elections. The stand out player was Glenn Maxwell with his unorthodox and powerful hitting, scoring 95, 89 and 95 in his first three innings with a strike rate of over 200 who got equal contribution from South African David Miller, both of them making the side look invincible.

There were many innings from the veteran Indian batsman Virender Sehwag and young star Manan Vohra which made the middle order batting easy and allowed the team to qualify for the playoffs. Due to a 122 run knock from Virender Sehwag against the Chennai Super Kings in the semifinal, KXIP made their way to the final. There they faced the Kolkata Knight Riders where they batted first and set a good target of 199 owing to Wriddhiman Saha's 115. However, due to Manish Pandey's 94 off 50 balls and his teammates' consistently high strike rate, including Piyush Chawla's 13 off five balls, KKR were able to win the final by three wickets in the final over of the match.

- 2014 CLT20

Kings XI Punjab qualified for the 2014 Champions League Twenty20 as they finished runners-up in the 2014 IPL. They were placed in Group B along with the Hobart Hurricanes (Australia), the Barbados Tridents (West Indies), the Cape Cobras (South Africa) and the Northern Knights (New Zealand).

Kings XI's first match was in their home stadium, the PCA Stadium, Mohali where they beat Hobart Hurricanes by five wickets, overhauling Hobart's 144–6 in 17.4 overs. Thisara Perera was named the Man Of The Match with 2–17 and 35. Glenn Maxwell top scored in the game with 43. They also won the second match beating the Barbados Tridents by four wickets. They won their third match of the competition against the Northern Knights and qualified for the semi finals.

They continued to win their final group match against the Cape Cobras but were knocked out of the tournament at the semi-final stage with a disappointing defeat against their IPL rivals the Chennai Super Kings, who went on to win the tournament.

- 2015 IPL season

George Bailey continued to lead the side during the 2015 season. The team won just three of the 14 games and finished eighth in the league. David Miller finished the season as top scorer with 357 runs and Anureet Singh finished the season as the top wicket taker with 15 wickets.

- 2016 IPL season

David Miller and Murali Vijay captained the team in the first and second half of the 2016 season respectively. The team finished eighth once again with only four wins. Murali Vijay was the top scorer with 453 runs and Sandeep Sharma was the top wicket taker with 15 wickets.

- 2017 IPL season

Virender Sehwag joined as head coach as the team looked to recover from two back-to-back last-place finishes in the league. Glenn Maxwell was appointed as the captain. Eoin Morgan, Darren Sammy and Hashim Amla joined the likes of David Miller in the team. The team missed out on a place in the play-offs by a last game defeat to the Rising Pune Supergiant and ended the season in fifth, winning seven out of their 14 games. Hashim Amla finished the season as top scorer with 420 runs including two centuries, and Sandeep Sharma was the top wicket taker with 17 wickets.

- 2018 IPL season

The Kings XI Punjab squad for the 2018 IPL season included internationals such as: Ravichandran Ashwin, Yuvraj Singh, KL Rahul, Aaron Finch and Chris Gayle. Ashwin was appointed as captain and Brad Hodge as coach. The Tournament started well with KL Rahul scoring a fine fifty off 14 balls to guide KXIP home against Daredevils. Riding on KL Rahul and Chris Gayle's red hot form at the top and Andrew Tye and Mujeeb Ur Rahman with the ball, the team went on to win 5 out of their first six games, eventually becoming favourites to the title. Their weakness in Indian core was however exposed as they could manage just one win in the next eight and ultimately not being qualified for the playoffs despite a dream start from the beginning.

- 2019 IPL season

Franchises confirmed the names of retained players for the 12th season of Indian Premier League. KXIP retained the following players for the 2019 season: KL Rahul, Chris Gayle, Andrew Tye, Mayank Agarwal, Ankit Rajpoot, Mujeeb Ur Rahman, Karun Nair, David Miller and Ravichandran Ashwin. On the auction day (18 December 2018), KXIP snapped up new 13 players: Varun Chakaravarthy, Sam Curran, Mohammed Shami, Prabhsimran Singh, Nicholas Pooran, Moises Henriques, Hardus Viljoen, Darshan Nalkande, Sarfaraz Khan, Arshdeep Singh, Agnivesh Ayachi, Harpreet Brar, and Murugan Ashwin. Kings XI Punjab ended up in sixth position in the league table. KL Rahul was the highest run scorer for the team with 593 runs in 14 matches.

- 2020 IPL season

Kings XI Punjab released Varun Chakravarthy, Andrew Tye, Sam Curran, Prabhsimran Singh (who was rebought), David Miller, Moises Henriques and Agnivesh Ayachi from their 2020 roster. They have bought Glenn Maxwell, Deepak Hooda, James Neesham, Prabhsimran Singh, Chris Jordan, Tanjinder Dhillon, Ravi Bishnoi, Ishan Porel, Sheldon Cottrell for their 2020 squad. The retained players include KL Rahul, Karun Nair, Mohammed Shami, Nicholas Pooran, Mujeeb Ur Rahman, Chris Gayle, Mandeep Singh, Mayank Agarwal, Hardus Viljoen, Darshan Nalkande, Sarfaraz Khan, Arshdeep Singh, Harpreet Brar and Murugan Ashwin.They also transferred their former skipper R Ashwin to Delhi Capitals and Rajasthan Royals traded their all rounder Krishnappa Gowtham to Kings XI Punjab successfully.

On 20 September, the Kings XI started their season campaign. KL Rahul, the Kings' new captain, elected to field first. This thrilling match ended in a tie. Delhi started with a win in the tournament, defeating Punjab's team in the Super Over. Delhi scored 157-runs for the loss of 8 wickets in 20 overs. The team had lost early wickets, but Marcus Stoinis' brilliant innings helped the Delhi Capitals to build a 157-run target. In response to 158 runs, Punjab also scored 157-runs in 20 overs on Mayank Agarwal's knock of 89 runs.

On 24 September, Kings XI Punjab won their first match of the season defeating Royal Challengers Bangalore by 97-runs. KL Rahul lost the toss and was put to bat. Rahul and Mayank Agarwal build the Kings XI innings with a 57-run stand for the first wicket. Rahul scored 132 off 69 balls with 14 fours and 7 sixes and helped the Kings XI finish the innings at 206/3 in 20 overs. Chasing a target of 207, the Royal Challengers had lost three wickets in a first four overs. Kings XI's new ball pair of Sheldon Cottrell and Mohammed Shami continued their good work from the first match and Royal Challengers were eventually bowled out for 109.

Rahul became the fastest Indian batsman to complete 2000 runs in IPL. However, they were ousted against Rajasthan Royals who successfully chased down 223 and then continued to lose five matches. The losing streak was broken when Punjab defeated Bangalore for 2nd time and then defeated Mumbai Indians in the Super Over and continued to win three more matches against Delhi, Hyderabad and Kolkata. However, they lost two matches at the end of the tournament. Their last match was against Chennai Super Kings who won comprehensively by 9 wickets, therefore knocking Punjab out of the tournament. They finished the season at the 6th place. KL Rahul was again the highest scorer for the team with 670 runs, while Mohammed Shami topped the bowling charts for the franchise, with 20 wickets from 14 matches.

CHAPTER THREE

Let's Know About Cricket

- *Cricket*

Cricket is a bat-and-ball game played between two teams of eleven players on a field at the centre of which is a 22-yard (20-metre) pitch with a wicket at each end, each comprising two bails balanced on three stumps. The game proceeds when a player on the fielding team, called the bowler, "bowls" (propels) the ball from one end of the pitch towards the wicket at the other end. The batting side's players score runs by striking the bowled ball with a bat and running between the wickets, while the bowling side tries to prevent this by keeping the ball within the field and getting it to either wicket, and dismiss each batter (so they are "out"). Means of dismissal include being bowled, when the ball hits the stumps and dislodges the bails, and by the fielding side either catching a hit ball before it touches the ground, or hitting a wicket with the ball before a batter can cross the crease line in front of the wicket to complete a run. When ten batters have been dismissed, the innings ends and the teams swap roles. The game is adjudicated by two umpires, aided by a third umpire and match referee in international matches.

Forms of cricket range from Twenty20, with each team batting for a single innings of 20 overs and the game generally lasting three hours, to Test matches played over five days. Traditionally cricketers play in all-white kit, but in limited overs cricket they wear club or team colours. In addition to the basic kit, some players wear protective gear to prevent injury caused by the ball, which is a hard, solid spheroid made of compressed leather with a slightly raised sewn seam enclosing a cork core layered with tightly wound string.

The earliest reference to cricket is in South East England in the mid-16th century. It spread globally with the expansion of the British Empire, with the first international matches in the second half of the 19th century. The game's governing body is the International Cricket Council (ICC), which has over 100 members, twelve of which are full members who play Test matches. The game's rules, the Laws of Cricket, are maintained by Marylebone Cricket Club (MCC) in London. The sport is followed primarily in South Asia, Australasia, the United Kingdom, southern Africa and the West Indies.Women's cricket, which is organised and played separately, has also achieved international standard. The most successful side playing international cricket is Australia, which has won seven One Day International trophies, including five World Cups, more than any other country and has been the top-rated Test side more than any other country.

- *History of cricket to 1725*

A medieval "club ball" game involving an underhand bowl towards a batter. Ball catchers are shown positioning themselves to catch a ball. Detail from the Canticles of Holy Mary, 13th century.

Cricket is one of many games in the "club ball" sphere that basically involve hitting a ball with a hand-held implement; others include baseball (which shares many similarities with cricket, both belonging in the more specific bat-and-ball games category), golf, hockey, tennis, squash, badminton and table tennis. In cricket's case, a key difference is the existence of a solid target structure, the wicket (originally, it is thought, a "wicket gate" through which sheep were herded), that the batter must defend. The cricket historian Harry Altham identified three "groups" of "club ball" games: the "hockey group", in which the ball is driven to and fro between two targets (the goals); the "golf group", in which the ball is driven towards an undefended target (the hole); and the "cricket group", in which "the ball is aimed at a mark (the wicket) and driven away from it".

It is generally believed that cricket originated as a children's game in the south-eastern counties of England, sometime during the medieval period.Although there are claims for prior dates, the earliest definite reference to cricket being played comes from evidence given at a court case in Guildford in January 1597 (Old Style), equating to January 1598 in the modern calendar. The case concerned ownership of a certain plot of land and the court heard the testimony of a 59-year-old coroner, John Derrick, who gave witness that.

Being a scholler in the ffree schoole of Guldeford hee and diverse of his fellows did runne and play there at creckett and other plaies.

Given Derrick's age, it was about half a century earlier when he was at school and so it is certain that cricket was being played c. 1550 by boys in Surrey. The view that it was originally a children's game is reinforced by Randle Cotgrave's 1611 English-French dictionary in which he defined the noun "crosse" as "the crooked staff wherewith boys play at cricket" and the verb form "crosser" as "to play at cricket".

One possible source for the sport's name is the Old English word "cryce" (or "cricc") meaning a crutch or staff. In Samuel Johnson's Dictionary, he derived cricket from "cryce, Saxon, a stick". In Old French, the word "criquet" seems to have meant a kind of club or stick. Given the strong medieval trade connections between south-east England and the County of Flanders when the latter belonged to the Duchy of Burgundy, the name may have been derived from the Middle Dutch (in use in Flanders at the time) "krick"(-e), meaning a stick (crook). Another possible source is the Middle Dutch word "krickstoel", meaning a long low stool used for kneeling in church and which resembled the long low wicket with two stumps used in early cricket. According to Heiner Gillmeister, a European language expert of Bonn University, "cricket" derives from the Middle Dutch phrase for hockey, met de (krik ket)sen (i.e., "with the stick chase"). Gillmeister has suggested that not only the name but also the sport itself may be of Flemish origin.

- *Growth of amateur and professional cricket in England*

Evolution of the cricket bat. The original "hockey stick" (left) evolved into the straight bat from c. 1760 when pitched delivery bowling began.

Although the main object of the game has always been to score the most runs, the early form of cricket differed from the modern game in certain key technical aspects; the North American variant of cricket known as wicket retained many of these aspects. The ball was bowled underarm by the bowler and along the ground towards a batter armed with a bat that in shape resembled a hockey stick; the batter defended a low, two-stump wicket; and runs were called notches because the scorers recorded them by notching tally sticks.

In 1611, the year Cotgrave's dictionary was published, ecclesiastical court records at Sidlesham in Sussex state that two parishioners, Bartholomew Wyatt and Richard Latter, failed to attend church on Easter Sunday because they were playing cricket. They were fined 12d each and ordered to do penance.This is the earliest mention of adult participation in cricket and it was around the same time that the earliest known organised inter-parish or village match was played – at Chevening, Kent. In 1624, a player called Jasper Vinall died after he was accidentally struck on the head during a match between two parish teams in Sussex.

Cricket remained a low-key local pursuit for much of the 17th century. It is known, through numerous references found in the records of ecclesiastical court cases, to have been proscribed at times by the Puritans before and during the Commonwealth. The problem was nearly always the issue of Sunday play as the Puritans considered cricket to be "profane" if played on the Sabbath, especially if large crowds or gambling were involved.

According to the social historian Derek Birley, there was a "great upsurge of sport after the Restoration" in 1660. Gambling on sport became a problem significant enough for Parliament to pass the 1664 Gambling Act, limiting stakes to £100 which was, in any case, a colossal sum exceeding the annual income of 99% of the population. Along with prizefighting, horse racing and blood sports, cricket was perceived to be a gambling sport.Rich patrons made matches for high stakes, forming teams in which they engaged the first professional players.By the end of the century, cricket had developed into a major sport that was spreading throughout England and was already being taken abroad by English mariners and colonisers – the earliest reference to cricket overseas is dated 1676. A 1697 newspaper report survives of "a great cricket match" played in Sussex "for fifty guineas apiece" – this is the earliest known contest that is generally considered a First Class match.

- The patrons, and other players from the social class known as the "gentry", began to classify themselves as "amateurs" to establish a clear distinction from the professionals, who were invariably members of the working class, even to the point of having separate changing and dining facilities. The gentry, including such high-ranking nobles as the Dukes of Richmond, exerted their honour code of noblesse oblige to claim rights of leadership in any sporting contests they took part in, especially as it was necessary for them to play alongside their "social inferiors" if they were to win their bets. In time, a perception took hold that the typical amateur who played in first-class cricket, until 1962 when amateurism was abolished, was someone with a public school education who had then gone to one of Cambridge or Oxford University – society insisted that such people were "officers and gentlemen" whose destiny was to provide leadership. In a purely financial sense, the cricketing amateur would theoretically claim expenses for playing while his professional counterpart played under contract and was paid a wage or match fee; in practice, many amateurs claimed more than actual expenditure and the derisive term "shamateur" was coined to describe the practice.

- *The Young Cricketer, 1768*

The game underwent major development in the 18th century to become England's national sport.Its success was underwritten by the twin necessities of patronage and betting. Cricket was prominent in London as early as 1707 and, in the middle years of the century, large crowds flocked to matches on the Artillery Ground in Finsbury. The single wicket form of the sport attracted huge crowds and wagers to match, its popularity peaking in the 1748 season. Bowling underwent an evolution around 1760 when bowlers began to pitch the ball instead of rolling or skimming it towards the batter. This caused a revolution in bat design because, to deal with the bouncing ball, it was necessary to introduce the modern straight bat in place of the old "hockey stick" shape.

The Hambledon Club was founded in the 1760s and, for the next twenty years until the formation of Marylebone Cricket Club (MCC) and the opening of Lord's Old Ground in 1787, Hambledon was both the game's greatest club and its focal point. MCC quickly became the sport's premier club and the custodian of the Laws of Cricket. New Laws introduced in the latter part of the 18th century included the three stump wicket and leg before wicket (lbw).

The 19th century saw underarm bowling superseded by first roundarm and then overarm bowling. Both developments were controversial.Organisation of the game at county level led to the creation of the county clubs, starting with Sussex in 1839. In December 1889, the eight leading county clubs formed the official County Championship, which began in 1890.

The most famous player of the 19th century was W. G. Grace, who started his long and influential career in 1865. It was especially during the career of Grace that the distinction between amateurs and professionals became blurred by the existence of players like him who were nominally amateur but, in terms of their financial gain, de facto professional. Grace himself was said to have been paid more money for playing cricket than any professional.

The last two decades before the First World War have been called the "Golden Age of cricket". It is a nostalgic name prompted by the collective sense of loss resulting from the war, but the period did produce some great players and memorable matches, especially as organised competition at county and Test level developed.

- *Cricket becomes an international sport*

In 1844, the first-ever international match took place between the United States and Canada. In 1859, a team of English players went to North America on the first overseas tour. Meanwhile, the British Empire had been instrumental in spreading the game overseas and by the middle of the 19th century it had become well established in Australia, the Caribbean, India, Pakistan, New Zealand, North America and South Africa.

In 1862, an English team made the first tour of Australia. The first Australian team to travel overseas consisted of Aboriginal stockmen who toured England in 1868. The first One Day International match was played on 5 January 1971 between Australia and England at the Melbourne Cricket Ground.

In 1876–77, an England team took part in what was retrospectively recognised as the first-ever Test match at the Melbourne Cricket Ground against Australia. The rivalry between England and Australia gave birth to The Ashes in 1882, and this has remained Test cricket's most famous contest. Test cricket began to expand in 1888–89 when South Africa played England.

- *World cricket in the 20th century*

The inter-war years were dominated by Australia's Don Bradman, statistically the greatest Test batter of all time. Test cricket continued to expand during the 20th century with the addition of the West Indies (1928), New Zealand (1930) and India (1932) before the Second World War and then Pakistan (1952), Sri Lanka (1982), Zimbabwe (1992), Bangladesh (2000), Ireland and Afghanistan (both 2018) in the post-war period. South Africa was banned from international cricket from 1970 to 1992 as part of the apartheid boycott.

- *The rise of limited overs cricket*

Cricket entered a new era in 1963 when English counties introduced the limited overs variant. As it was sure to produce a result, limited overs cricket was lucrative and the number of matches increased. The first Limited Overs International was played in 1971 and the governing International Cricket Council (ICC), seeing its potential, staged the first limited overs Cricket World Cup in 1975. In the 21st century, a new limited overs form, Twenty20, made an immediate impact. On 22 June 2017, Afghanistan and Ireland became the 11th and 12th ICC full members, enabling them to play Test cricket.

- *A typical cricket field.*

In cricket, the rules of the game are specified in a code called The Laws of Cricket (hereinafter called "the Laws") which has a global remit. There are 42 Laws (always written with a capital "L"). The earliest known version of the code was drafted in 1744 and, since 1788, it has been owned and maintained by its custodian, the Marylebone Cricket Club (MCC) in London.

- Playing area

Cricket is a bat-and-ball game played on a cricket field between two teams of eleven players each. The field is usually circular or oval in shape and the edge of the playing area is marked by a boundary, which may be a fence, part of the stands, a rope, a painted line or a combination of these; the boundary must if possible be marked along its entire length.

In the approximate centre of the field is a rectangular pitch (see image, below) on which a wooden target called a wicket is sited at each end; the wickets are placed 22 yards (20 m) apart. The pitch is a flat surface 10 feet (3.0 m) wide, with very short grass that tends to be worn away as the game progresses (cricket can also be played on artificial surfaces, notably matting). Each wicket is made of three wooden stumps topped by two bails.

- Cricket pitch and creases

As illustrated above, the pitch is marked at each end with four white painted lines: a bowling crease, a popping crease and two return creases. The three stumps are aligned centrally on the bowling crease, which is eight feet eight inches long. The popping crease is drawn four feet in front of the bowling crease and parallel to it; although it is drawn as a twelve-foot line (six feet either side of the wicket), it is, in fact, unlimited in length. The return creases are drawn at right angles to the popping crease so that they intersect the ends of the bowling crease; each return crease is drawn as an eight-foot line, so that it extends four feet behind the bowling crease, but is also, in fact, unlimited in length.

Before a match begins, the team captains (who are also players) toss a coin to decide which team will bat first and so take the first innings. Innings is the term used for each phase of play in the match.In each innings, one team bats, attempting to score runs, while the other team bowls and fields the ball, attempting to restrict the scoring and dismiss the batters. When the first innings ends, the teams change roles; there can be two to four innings depending upon the type of match. A match with four scheduled innings is played over three to five days; a match with two scheduled innings is usually completed in a single day. During an innings, all eleven members of the fielding team take the field, but usually only two members of the batting team are on the field at any given time.

The exception to this is if a batter has any type of illness or injury restricting his or her ability to run, in this case the batter is allowed a runner who can run between the wickets when the batter hits a scoring run or runs,though this does not apply in international cricket. The order of batters is usually announced just before the match, but it can be varied.

The main objective of each team is to score more runs than their opponents but, in some forms of cricket, it is also necessary to dismiss all of the opposition batters in their final innings in order to win the match, which would otherwise be drawn. If the team batting last is all out having scored fewer runs than their opponents, they are said to have "lost by n runs" (where n is the difference between the aggregate number of runs scored by the teams). If the team that bats last scores enough runs to win, it is said to have "won by n wickets", where n is the number of wickets left to fall. For example, a team that passes its opponents‘ total having lost six wickets (i.e., six of their batters have been dismissed) have won the match "by four wickets".

In a two-innings-a-side match, one team's combined first and second innings total may be less than the other side's first innings total. The team with the greater score is then said to have "won by an innings and n runs", and does not need to bat again: n is the difference between the two teams' aggregate scores. If the team batting last is all out, and both sides have scored the same number of runs, then the match is a tie; this result is quite rare in matches of two innings a side with only 62 happening in first-class matches from the earliest known instance in 1741 until January 2017. In the traditional form of the game, if the time allotted for the match expires before either side can win, then the game is declared a draw.

If the match has only a single innings per side, then a maximum number of overs applies to each innings. Such a match is called a "limited overs" or "one-day" match, and the side scoring more runs wins regardless of the number of wickets lost, so that a draw cannot occur. In some cases, ties are broken by having each team bat for a one-over innings known as a Super Over; subsequent Super Overs may be played if the first Super Over ends in a tie. If this kind of match is temporarily interrupted by bad weather, then a complex mathematical formula, known as the Duckworth–Lewis–Stern method after its developers, is often used to recalculate a new target score. A one-day match can also be declared a "no-result" if fewer than a previously agreed number of overs have been bowled by either team, in circumstances that make normal resumption of play impossible; for example, wet weather.

In all forms of cricket, the umpires can abandon the match if bad light or rain makes it impossible to continue. There have been instances of entire matches, even Test matches scheduled to be played over five days, being lost to bad weather without a ball being bowled: for example, the third Test of the 1970/71 series in Australia.

- Innings

The innings (ending with 's' in both singular and plural form) is the term used for each phase of play during a match. Depending on the type of match being played, each team has either one or two innings. Sometimes all eleven members of the batting side take a turn to bat but, for various reasons, an innings can end before they have all done so. The innings terminates if the batting team is "all out", a term defined by the Laws: "at the fall of a wicket or the retirement of a batter, further balls remain to be bowled but no further batter is available to come in". In this situation, one of the batters has not been dismissed and is termed not out; this is because he has no partners left and there must always be two active batters while the innings is in progress.

- An innings may end early while there are still two not out batters

the batting team's captain may declare the innings closed even though some of his players have not had a turn to bat: this is a tactical decision by the captain, usually because he believes his team have scored sufficient runs and need time to dismiss the opposition in their innings

the set number of overs (i.e., in a limited overs match) have been bowled

the match has ended prematurely due to bad weather or running out of time

in the final innings of the match, the batting side has reached its target and won the game.

- Overs

The Laws state that, throughout an innings, "the ball shall be bowled from each end alternately in overs of 6 balls". The name "over" came about because the umpire calls "Over!" when six balls have been bowled. At this point, another bowler is deployed at the other end, and the fielding side changes ends while the batters do not. A bowler cannot bowl two successive overs, although a bowler can (and usually does) bowl alternate overs, from the same end, for several overs which are termed a "spell". The batters do not change ends at the end of the over, and so the one who was non-striker is now the striker and vice versa. The umpires also change positions so that the one who was at "square leg" now stands behind the wicket at the non-striker's end and vice versa.

- Clothing and equipment

English cricketer W. G. Grace "taking guard" in 1883. His pads and bat are very similar to those used today. The gloves have evolved somewhat. Many modern players use more defensive equipment than were available to Grace, most notably helmets and arm guards.

The wicket-keeper (a specialised fielder behind the batter) and the batters wear protective gear because of the hardness of the ball, which can be delivered at speeds of more than 145 kilometres per hour (90 mph) and presents a major health and safety concern.

Protective clothing includes pads (designed to protect the knees and shins), batting gloves or wicket-keeper's gloves for the hands, a safety helmet for the head and a box for male players inside the trousers (to protect the crotch area). Some batters wear additional padding inside their shirts and trousers such as thigh pads, arm pads, rib protectors and shoulder pads. The only fielders allowed to wear protective gear are those in positions very close to the batter (i.e., if they are alongside or in front of him), but they cannot wear gloves or external leg guards.

Subject to certain variations, on-field clothing generally includes a collared shirt with short or long sleeves; long trousers; woolen pullover (if needed); cricket cap (for fielding) or a safety helmet; and spiked shoes or boots to increase traction. The kit is traditionally all white and this remains the case in Test and first-class cricket but, in limited overs cricket, team colours are worn instead.

- Bat and ball

Two types of cricket ball, both of the same size:

i) A used white ball. White balls are mainly used in limited overs cricket, especially in matches played at night, under floodlights (left).

ii) A used red ball. Red balls are used in Test cricket, first-class cricket and some other forms of cricket (right).

The essence of the sport is that a bowler delivers (i.e., bowls) the ball from his or her end of the pitch towards the batter who, armed with a bat, is "on strike" at the other end (see next sub-section: Basic gameplay).

The bat is made of wood, usually Salix alba (white willow), and has the shape of a blade topped by a cylindrical handle. The blade must not be more than 4.25 inches (10.8 cm) wide and the total length of the bat not more than 38 inches (97 cm). There is no standard for the weight, which is usually between 2 lb 7 oz and 3 lb (1.1 and 1.4 kg).

The ball is a hard leather-seamed spheroid, with a circumference of 9 inches (23 cm). The ball has a "seam": six rows of stitches attaching the leather shell of the ball to the string and cork interior. The seam on a new ball is prominent and helps the bowler propel it in a less predictable manner. During matches, the quality of the ball deteriorates to a point where it is no longer usable; during the course of this deterioration, its behaviour in flight will change and can influence the outcome of the match. Players will, therefore, attempt to modify the ball's behaviour by modifying its physical properties. Polishing the ball and wetting it with sweat or saliva is legal, even when the polishing is deliberately done on one side only to increase the ball's swing through the air, but the acts of rubbing other substances into the ball, scratching the surface or picking at the seam are illegal ball tampering.

- Player roles

Basic gameplay: bowler to batter

During normal play, thirteen players and two umpires are on the field. Two of the players are batters and the rest are all eleven members of the fielding team. The other nine players in the batting team are off the field in the pavilion. The image with overlay below shows what is happening when a ball is being bowled and which of the personnel are on or close to the pitch.

- Return crease

In the photo, the two batters (3 & 8; wearing yellow) have taken position at each end of the pitch (6). Three members of the fielding team (4, 10 & 11; wearing dark blue) are in shot. One of the two umpires (1; wearing white hat) is stationed behind the wicket (2) at the bowler's (4) end of the pitch. The bowler (4) is bowling the ball (5) from his end of the pitch to the batter at the other end who is called the "striker". The other batter (3) at the bowling end is called the "non-striker". The wicket-keeper (10), who is a specialist, is positioned behind the striker's wicket (9) and behind him stands one of the fielders in a position called "first slip" (11). While the bowler and the first slip are wearing conventional kit only, the two batters and the wicket-keeper are wearing protective gear including safety helmets, padded gloves and leg guards (pads).

While the umpire (1) in shot stands at the bowler's end of the pitch, his colleague stands in the outfield, usually in or near the fielding position called "square leg", so that he is in line with the popping crease (7) at the striker's end of the pitch. The bowling crease (not numbered) is the one on which the wicket is located between the return creases (12). The bowler (4) intends to hit the wicket (9) with the ball (5) or, at least, to prevent the striker (8) from scoring runs. The striker (8) intends, by using his bat, to defend his wicket and, if possible, to hit the ball away from the pitch in order to score runs.

Some players are skilled in both batting and bowling, or as either or these as well as wicket-keeping, so are termed all-rounders. Bowlers are classified according to their style, generally as fast bowlers, seam bowlers or spinners. Batters are classified according to whether they are right-handed or left-handed.

- Fielding

Of the eleven fielders, three are in shot in the image above. The other eight are elsewhere on the field, their positions determined on a tactical basis by the captain or the bowler. Fielders often change position between deliveries, again as directed by the captain or bowler.

If a fielder is injured or becomes ill during a match, a substitute is allowed to field instead of him, but the substitute cannot bowl or act as a captain, except in the case of concussion substitutes in international cricket. The substitute leaves the field when the injured player is fit to return. The Laws of Cricket were updated in 2017 to allow substitutes to act as wicket-keepers.

- Bowling and dismissal

Glenn McGrath of Australia holds the world record for most wickets in the Cricket World Cup.

Most bowlers are considered specialists in that they are selected for the team because of their skill as a bowler, although some are all-rounders and even specialist batters bowl occasionally. The specialists bowl several times during an innings but may not bowl two overs consecutively. If the captain wants a bowler to "change ends", another bowler must temporarily fill in so that the change is not immediate.

A bowler reaches his delivery stride by means of a "run-up" and an over is deemed to have begun when the bowler starts his run-up for the first delivery of that over, the ball then being "in play".

Fast bowlers, needing momentum, take a lengthy run up while bowlers with a slow delivery take no more than a couple of steps before bowling. The fastest bowlers can deliver the ball at a speed of over 145 kilometres per hour (90 mph) and they sometimes rely on sheer speed to try to defeat the batter, who is forced to react very quickly.

Other fast bowlers rely on a mixture of speed and guile by making the ball seam or swing (i.e. curve) in flight. This type of delivery can deceive a batter into miscuing his shot, for example, so that the ball just touches the edge of the bat and can then be "caught behind" by the wicket-keeper or a slip fielder. At the other end of the bowling scale is the spin bowler who bowls at a relatively slow pace and relies entirely on guile to deceive the batter. A spinner will often "buy his wicket" by "tossing one up" (in a slower, steeper parabolic path) to lure the batter into making a poor shot. The batter has to be very wary of such deliveries as they are often "flighted" or spun so that the ball will not behave quite as he expects and he could be "trapped" into getting himself out. In between the pacemen and the spinners are the medium paced seamers who rely on persistent accuracy to try to contain the rate of scoring and wear down the batter's concentration.

There are nine ways in which a batter can be dismissed: five relatively common and four extremely rare. The common forms of dismissal are bowled, caught, leg before wicket (lbw), run out and stumped. Rare methods are hit wicket,hit the ball twice, obstructing the field and timed out. The Laws state that the fielding team, usually the bowler in practice, must appeal for a dismissal before the umpire can give his decision. If the batter is out, the umpire raises a forefinger and says "Out!"; otherwise, he will shake his head and say "Not out".There is, effectively, a tenth method of dismissal, retired out, which is not an on-field dismissal as such but rather a retrospective one for which no fielder is credited.

- Batting, runs and extras

The directions in which a right-handed batter, facing down the page, intends to send the ball when playing various cricketing shots. The diagram for a left-handed batter is a mirror image of this one.

Batters take turns to bat via a batting order which is decided beforehand by the team captain and presented to the umpires, though the order remains flexible when the captain officially nominates the team. Substitute batters are generally not allowed, except in the case of concussion substitutes in international cricket.

In order to begin batting the batter first adopts a batting stance. Standardly, this involves adopting a slight crouch with the feet pointing across the front of the wicket, looking in the direction of the bowler, and holding the bat so it passes over the feet and so its tip can rest on the ground near to the toes of the back foot.

A skilled batter can use a wide array of "shots" or "strokes" in both defensive and attacking mode. The idea is to hit the ball to the best effect with the flat surface of the bat's blade. If the ball touches the side of the bat it is called an "edge". The batter does not have to play a shot and can allow the ball to go through to the wicketkeeper. Equally, he does not have to attempt a run when he hits the ball with his bat. Batters do not always seek to hit the ball as hard as possible, and a good player can score runs just by making a deft stroke with a turn of the wrists or by simply "blocking" the ball but directing it away from fielders so that he has time to take a run. A wide variety of shots are played, the batter's repertoire including strokes named according to the style of swing and the direction aimed: e.g., "cut", "drive", "hook", "pull".

The batter on strike (i.e. the "striker") must prevent the ball hitting the wicket, and try to score runs by hitting the ball with his bat so that he and his partner have time to run from one end of the pitch to the other before the fielding side can return the ball. To register a run, both runners must touch the ground behind the popping crease with either their bats or their bodies (the batters carry their bats as they run). Each completed run increments the score of both the team and the striker.

- Sachin Tendulkar is the only player to have scored one hundred international centuries

The decision to attempt a run is ideally made by the batter who has the better view of the ball's progress, and this is communicated by calling: usually "yes", "no" or "wait". More than one run can be scored from a single hit: hits worth one to three runs are common, but the size of the field is such that it is usually difficult to run four or more. To compensate for this, hits that reach the boundary of the field are automatically awarded four runs if the ball touches the ground en route to the boundary or six runs if the ball clears the boundary without touching the ground within the boundary. In these cases the batters do not need to run. Hits for five are unusual and generally rely on the help of "overthrows" by a fielder returning the ball. If an odd number of runs is scored by the striker, the two batters have changed ends, and the one who was non-striker is now the striker. Only the striker can score individual runs, but all runs are added to the team's total.

Additional runs can be gained by the batting team as extras (called "sundries" in Australia) due to errors made by the fielding side. This is achieved in four ways: no-ball, a penalty of one extra conceded by the bowler if he breaks the rules; wide, a penalty of one extra conceded by the bowler if he bowls so that the ball is out of the batter's reach bye, an extra awarded if the batter misses the ball and it goes past the wicket-keeper and gives the batters time to run in the conventional way leg bye, as for a bye except that the ball has hit the batter's body, though not his bat. If the bowler has conceded a no-ball or a wide, his team incurs an additional penalty because that ball (i.e., delivery) has to be bowled again and hence the batting side has the opportunity to score more runs from this extra ball.

- Specialist roles

Captain (cricket) and Wicket-keeper

The captain is often the most experienced player in the team, certainly the most tactically astute, and can possess any of the main skillsets as a batter, a bowler or a wicket-keeper. Within the Laws, the captain has certain responsibilities in terms of nominating his players to the umpires before the match and ensuring that his players conduct themselves "within the spirit and traditions of the game as well as within the Laws".

The wicket-keeper (sometimes called simply the "keeper") is a specialist fielder subject to various rules within the Laws about his equipment and demeanour. He is the only member of the fielding side who can effect a stumping and is the only one permitted to wear gloves and external leg guards. Depending on their primary skills, the other ten players in the team tend to be classified as specialist batters or specialist bowlers. Generally, a team will include five or six specialist batters and four or five specialist bowlers, plus the wicket-keeper.

- Umpires and scorers

Umpire (cricket), Scoring (cricket), and Cricket statistics

An umpire signals a decision to the scorers

The game on the field is regulated by the two umpires, one of whom stands behind the wicket at the bowler's end, the other in a position called "square leg" which is about 15–20 metres away from the batter on strike and in line with the popping crease on which he is taking guard. The umpires have several responsibilities including adjudication on whether a ball has been correctly bowled (i.e., not a no-ball or a wide); when a run is scored; whether a batter is out (the fielding side must first appeal to the umpire, usually with the phrase "How's that?" or "Owzat?"); when intervals start and end; and the suitability of the pitch, field and weather for playing the game. The umpires are authorised to interrupt or even abandon a match due to circumstances likely to endanger the players, such as a damp pitch or deterioration of the light.

Off the field in televised matches, there is usually a third umpire who can make decisions on certain incidents with the aid of video evidence. The third umpire is mandatory under the playing conditions for Test and Limited Overs International matches played between two ICC full member countries. These matches also have a match referee whose job is to ensure that play is within the Laws and the spirit of the game.

The match details, including runs and dismissals, are recorded by two official scorers, one representing each team. The scorers are directed by the hand signals of an umpire . For example, the umpire raises a forefinger to signal that the batter is out (has been dismissed); he raises both arms above his head if the batter has hit the ball for six runs. The scorers are required by the Laws to record all runs scored, wickets taken and overs bowled; in practice, they also note significant amounts of additional data relating to the game.

A match's statistics are summarised on a scorecard. Prior to the popularisation of scorecards, most scoring was done by men sitting on vantage points cuttings notches on tally sticks and runs were originally called notches.According to Rowland Bowen, the earliest known scorecard templates were introduced in 1776 by T. Pratt of Sevenoaks and soon came into general use.It is believed that scorecards were printed and sold at Lord's for the first time in 1846.

- *thank you for buy & read this book*

have a great day of your
from : Mr Vivek Kumar Pandey

9 798885 308045

Printed by Libri Plureos GmbH in Hamburg, Germany